VIOLA EDITIO
BOOK TWO

MW00782866

Orchestra
Expressions

Lead Author: **Kathleen DeBerry Brungard**
Authors: **Michael L. Alexander**   **Gerald E. Anderson**   **Sandra Dackow**
Contributing Editor: **Anne C. Witt**
Contributing Arrangers: **Jack Bullock, Victor Lopez, Tom Roed**

--- Art Credits ---

The World of the Naïve by Max Ernst (1891–1976) Oil on canvas. Photo: Georges Meguerditc. Musée National d'Art Moderne, Centre Georges Pompidou, Paris, France. Photo Credit: CNAC/MNAM/Dist. Réunion des Musées Nationaux/Art Resource, NY
Student page: 6

Fan Quilt, Mt. Carmel, Jan. 16, 1893, made by Residents of Bourbon County, Kentucky. Cotton, wool, silk, velvet, lace, ribbon, silk thread, paint, chromolithographic paper decals, and canvas. 85 x 72 1/4 in. (215.9 x 183.5 cm). © Smithsonian American Art Museum, Washington, D.C./Art Resource, NY.
Student page: 12

Eggs Encircled by Carlotta M. Corpron (1948). Gelatin silver print, 9 9/16 x 7 13/16 in. © 1988, Amon Carter Museum, Fort Worth, Texas. Gift of the artist.
Student page: 18

The Love Song by Alexei Stiepanoff. Eaton Gallery, Princes Arcade, London, Great Britain. Photo Credit: Fine Art Photographic Library, London / Art Resource, NY.
Student page: 22

Deluge 1980 by Gail Butt (b. 1924). Watercolor on paper. 26 x 39 in. Reprinted with the artist's permission. Transparency credit: Sheldon Memorial Art Gallery, University of Nebraska-Lincoln, F. M. Hall collection.
Student page: 26

Illustration to "Wilhelm Tell" by Friedrich Schiller (1805). Act 3, Scene 3: The Shooting of the Apple. Colored aquatinta, ca. 1820. Photo: Dietmar Katz. Kunstbibliothek, Staatliche Museen zu Berlin, Berlin, Germany. Photo Credit: Bildarchiv Preussischer Kulturbesitz/Art Resource, NY
Student page: 32

The Starry Night (1889) by Vincent Van Gogh (1853–1890). Oil on canvas, 29 x 36 in. Acquired through the Lillie P. Bliss Bequest. (472.19) Museum of Modern Art, New York, NY, USA. Digital Image © The Museum of Modern Art/Licensed by SCALA/Art Resource, NY.
Student page: 38

Gauchos mounted on horses using bolas to hunt rhea, the flightless bird. Chromolithograph. Private collection. Photo Credit: Image Select/Art Resource, NY
Student page: 44

COURTESY OF Lucasfilm Ltd.
Star Wars: Episode IV - A New Hope
© 1977 and 1997 Lucasfilm Ltd. & ™.
All rights reserved. Used under authorization.
Unauthorized duplication is a violation of applicable law.
Student page: 51

Warm-ups CD 1:3

Creative Tools of Music

Dynamics—terms or symbols used to notate a sound level or change of sound level

Interval—the distance between two pitches

Vibrato—a technique for vibrating the sound to create a warm, rich tone

f **Forte**—play loudly   *p* **Piano**—play softly

Rhythm Chart 1

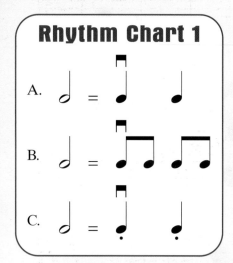

Tone Variables

Dynamic	Bow Speed	Bow Weight	Sound Point	Bow Placement
f	Fast	Heavy	Closer to the bridge	Lower half
p	Slow	Light	Closer to the fingerboard	Upper half

1 D Major Scale (Round)

2 D Major Arpeggio

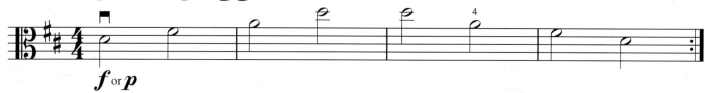

3 D Major Thirds (Round)

4 Intervals

Keep fingers down on the A string.

5 Hopp, Hopp, Hopp   CD 1:4

Folk Song, Germany

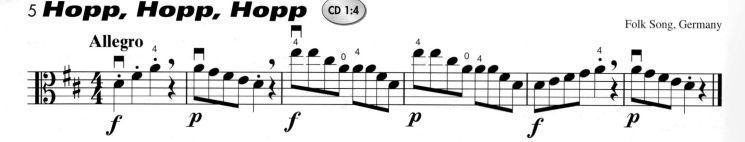

6 Bow Speed in 4/4

Slow   Fast   Slow   Fast

f–p

7 Etude

CD 1:5

IGNACE PLEYEL, Austria

Moderato

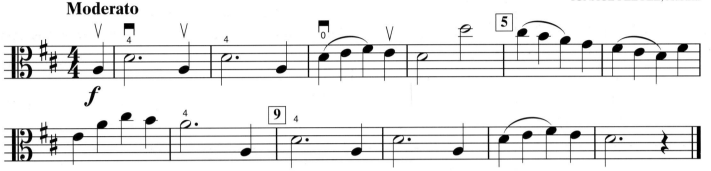

f

8 Bow Speed in 3/4

Slow   Fast   Slow   Fast

f–p

9 Bow Speed Waltz

GERALD ANDERSON, U.S.A.

Allegro

f

Fine

D.C. al Fine

Ear Training Expression—Worksheet #2

Creative Expression—Improvise over the I chord in D Major (Worksheet #3)

CD 1:55

Orchestra @ Home

LESSON 1

Perform orchestra and vibrato warm-ups to CD 1:3.

Practice Lines 1–3. Focus on intonation and tone variables.

Perform Line 4 with singing, pizzicato, and arco.

Practice Line 5 using same bow speed and different bow weights.

LESSON 2

1. Perform orchestra and vibrato warm-ups to CD 1:3.

2. Practice Lines 6 and 8. Focus on bow speed/weight, consistent dynamics, and good tone quality.

3. Perform Line 7 with good tone. Teach Tone Variables to family and friends.

LESSON 3

1. Perform orchestra and vibrato warm-ups to CD 1:3.

2. Practice Line 9. Teach bow speed/weight and dynamics to family and friends.

3. Improvise with notes of the D Major chord. CD 1:55.

Warm-ups CD 1:3

Creative Tools of Music

Crescendo (cresc.)—play gradually louder

Decrescendo (decresc., diminuendo, dim.)—play gradually soft

mf Mezzo Forte—play moderately loudly; softer than forte

mp Mezzo Piano—play moderately softly; louder than piano

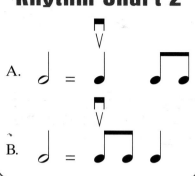

Rhythm Chart 2

Rhythm Chart 3

10 G Major Scale #1 (Round)

11 G Major Arpeggio #1

12 G Major Thirds #1 (Round)

13 Jingli Nona CD 1:6

Folk Song, Malaysia

Moderato

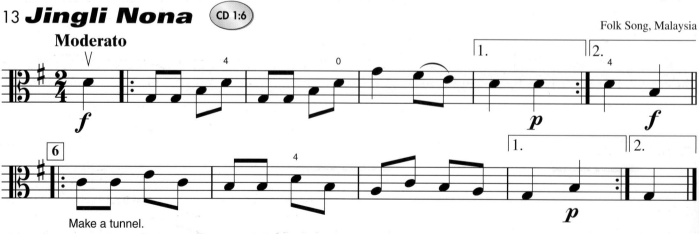

Make a tunnel.

 Ear Training Expression—Worksheet #2

Creative Expression—Composition #1 (Worksheet #4)

14 G Major Scale #2 (Round)

15 G Major Arpeggio #2

16 G Major Thirds #2 (Round)

17 I Don't Know You*   CD 1:7

Singing Game, Poland

Allegro

18 Imbabura   CD 1:8

Folk Song, Ecuador

Allegro

Orchestra @ Home

LESSON 1

Perform orchestra and vibrato warm-ups to CD 1:3.

Practice Lines 10–12 using Rhythm Chart #2. Focus on dynamics.

Practice and perform Line 13 with clapping, pizzicato, and arco. Focus on dynamics in 1st and 2nd endings.

Work on your composition.

LESSON 2

1. Perform orchestra and vibrato warm-ups to CD 1:3.

2. Perform Lines 13 and 17. Focus on proper dynamics.

3. Sight-read Line 18 without stopping.

4. Complete and practice your composition.

5. Practice lines 14–16 using Rhythm Chart #3.

LESSON 3

1. Perform orchestra and vibrato warm-ups to CD 1:3.

2. Perform Lines 13, 17, and 18. Teach the origin of the songs to family and friends.

3. Memorize Lines 10 and 17.

5

Warm-ups *CD 1:3*

Creative Tools of Music

Suite—a collection of musical movements or dances

The World of the Naïve
by Max Ernst (1891-1976)
Photo Credit: CNAC/MNAM/Dist. Réunion des Musées
Nationaux/Art Resource, NY

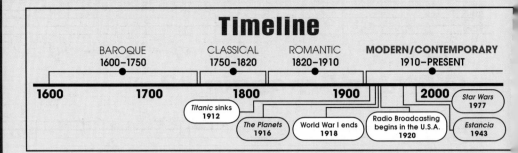

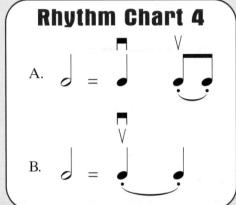

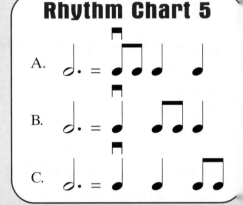

PORTRAIT

Gustav Holst

Gustav Holst was born in Cheltenham, England, in 1874 and died in London in 1934. He played the organ and the trombone and was well known as a music teacher at both the secondary school and university levels. English folk music, oriental themes, and Hindu literature influenced his work. *The Planets* is considered to be his greatest composition.

The Planets

The Planets is a suite for large orchestra consisting of a movement for each of the seven planets. Earth was not included and Pluto had yet to be discovered! Holst tried to capture in music a description of each planet and the personality of the mythological god for which it was named. The full title, "Jupiter, the Bringer of Jollity," refers to the leader of the gods of Roman mythology. *The Planets* is programmatic music composed in the Romantic style, and written in the 20th century.

19 *C Major Scale #1 (Round)*

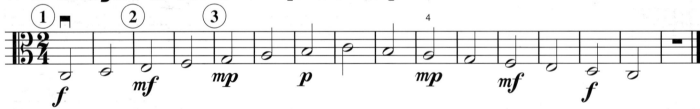

20 *C Major Arpeggio #1*

21 *C Major Thirds #1 (Round)*

22 Mattachins (Sword Dance)* CD 1:9

Allegro

Renaissance Dance, France

Ear Training Expression—Worksheet #2

23 C Major Scale #2 (Round)

24 C Major Arpeggio #2

25 C Major Thirds #2 (Round)

26 Jupiter* (From *The Planets*) CD 1:10

Andante

GUSTAV HOLST, England

Creative Expression—Improvise Movement to "Jupiter" from *The Planets*

Orchestra @ Home Your teacher will give you your lesson assignment.

7

Warm-ups CD 1:11

Creative Tools of Music

♪ Eighth Note—a note one half the value of a quarter note

❜ Eighth Rest—a rest one half the value of a quarter rest

Variation—a musical form; a restatement that retains some features of the original idea or theme

27 *Eighth Notes and Eighth Rests*

28 *Short Twins*

29 *The Cuckoo** CD 1:12

Folk Song, Italy, Switzerland

Allegro

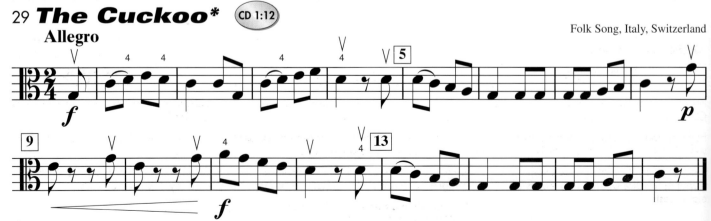

Ear Training Expression—Worksheet #2

30 **A Tricky Twinkle** (CD 1:13)
(Based on "Twinkle, Twinkle, Little Star")

Music by Monsieur BOUIN, France
Words by JANE and ANN TAYLOR, England

31 **Hi-Ho Mary-Oh (Round)**

Folk Song, England

 Creative Expression—Arrangement #1 (Worksheet #8)

32 **Avoid an Accident**

GERALD ANDERSON, U.S.A.

 **Orchestra @ Home**

LESSON 1

Perform orchestra and vibrato warm-ups to CD 1:11.

Perform Lines 27 and 28 counting aloud with clapping, pizzicato, and arco.

Practice Line 29 counting aloud with clapping, pizzicato, and arco. Focus on eighth rests.

LESSON 2

1. Perform orchestra and vibrato warm-ups to CD 1:11.

2. Practice Lines 30 and 31 counting aloud as you shadow bow and play arco.

3. Practice and perform Line 29. Focus on eighth notes/rests, dynamics, and bowing.

4. Complete the rhythmic variation on Worksheet #8.

LESSON 3

1. Perform orchestra and vibrato warm-ups to CD 1:11.

2. Perform Lines 30 and 31, counting the rhythms aloud.

3. Practice Line 32, counting the rhythms carefully. Focus on bowing.

Warm-ups CD 1:11

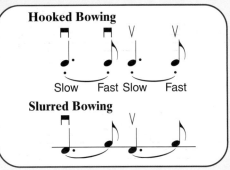

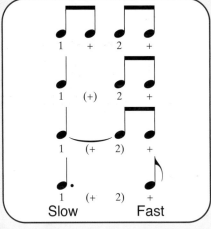

Creative Tools of Music

Dot—a dot after a note adds one half the value of the note

Dotted Quarter Note—a note that receives one and a half beats of sound in 4/4, 3/4 or 2/4 time

33 Dotted Quarter and Eighth Notes

34 March of the Dots CD 1:14

GERALD ANDERSON, U.S.A.

Creative Expression—Improvise over the V chord in D Major (Worksheet #11) CD 1:56

Ear Training Expression—Worksheet #2

Orchestra @ Home Your teacher will give you your lesson assignment.

35 **America***
(My Country 'Tis of Thee)   CD 1:15

Traditional Melody
Words by SAMUEL FRANCIS SMITH
American Patriotic, U.S.A.

36 **Arirang**   CD 1:16

Folk Song, Korea

37 **Kiowa Love Song**   CD 1:17

Native American Song, North America

Creative Expression—Composition #2 (Worksheet #15)

Ear Training Expression—Worksheet #2

38 **Scotland the Brave**   CD 1:18

Bagpipe Tune, Scotland

11

Warm-ups CD 1:11

Creative Tools of Music

Largo—a very slow tempo

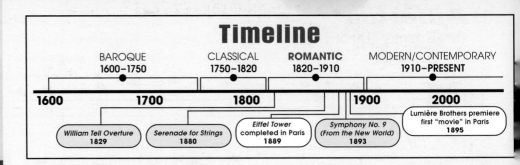

Timeline

BAROQUE 1600–1750	CLASSICAL 1750–1820	**ROMANTIC** 1820–1910	MODERN/CONTEMPORARY 1910–PRESENT

1600   **1700**   **1800**   **1900**   **2000**

- William Tell Overture 1829
- Serenade for Strings 1880
- Eiffel Tower completed in Paris 1889
- Symphony No. 9 (From the New World) 1893
- Lumière Brothers premiere first "movie" in Paris 1895

Fan Quilt, Mt. Carmel,
Jan. 16, 1893, made by Residents of
Bourbon County, Kentucky
© Smithsonian American Art Museum, Washington, D.C./Art Resource, NY.

PORTRAIT

Antonín Dvořák

Antonín Dvořák was born in Bohemia (now the Czech Republic) in 1841 and died in Prague, Czechoslovakia in 1904. He lived most of his life in the city of Prague where he was a successful composer and organist. He also played the violin and viola. At the height of his fame he was invited to head the newly-founded National Conservatory of Music in New York City. Dvořák spent three years in America and wrote some of his most famous music during that time. He was fascinated with the music of both African Americans and Native Americans. Dvořák spent a happy summer in Spillville, Iowa, where he played the organ, enjoyed the "wild west" shows that passed through town, and took early morning walks along the river to inspire musical ideas. In the absence of paper, he often jotted down ideas for themes on his shirt cuffs, making them terribly difficult to clean! He wrote keyboard music, nine symphonies, dozens of chamber music pieces, and numerous large choral compositions.

 Creative Expression—Theory #1 (Worksheet #17)

39 Las Mañanitas CD 1:19

Folk Song, Mexico

40 America, the Beautiful*
(Orchestra Arrangement)

Words by KATHARINE LEE BATES, U.S.A.
Music by SAMUEL AUGUSTUS WARD, U.S.A.
Arranged by SANDRA DACKOW, U.S.A.

CD 1:20

41 "Largo" From Symphony No. 9*
(From the New World)

CD 1:21

ANTONÍN DVOŘÁK, Czech Republic

Ear Training Expression—Worksheet #2

Creative Expression—Improvise movement to the Masterwork

Orchestra @ Home

LESSON 1

- Perform orchestra and vibrato warm-ups to CD 1:11.
- Practice Line 39. Focus on rhythm, bowing, and the key signature.
- Practice the melody of Line 40 and learn the orchestra part.

LESSON 2

1. Perform orchestra and vibrato warm-ups to CD 1:11.
2. Practice Lines 39–41. Focus on rhythms and bowings. Practice the orchestra part for Line 40. Focus on rhythm and intonation.
3. Memorize Line 41 using patterns to help you.
4. Complete Worksheet #18.

LESSON 3

1. Perform orchestra and vibrato warm-ups to CD 1:11.
2. Perform three pieces from Unit 7. Apply tone variables to create various dynamics.
3. Teach what you learned about Dvořák and Symphony No.9 to family and friends.

Warm-ups CD 1:22

Key of A Major

Rhythm Chart 6

A.

B.

C.

New Finger Pattern on the G String

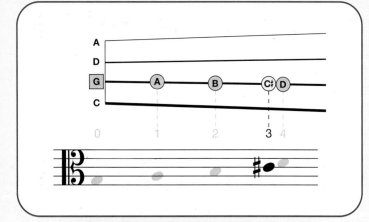

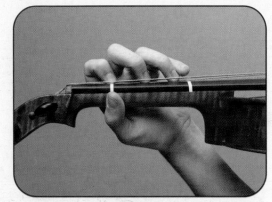

C# on the G string—3 Fingers Down
3–4 Pattern

New Finger Pattern on the D String

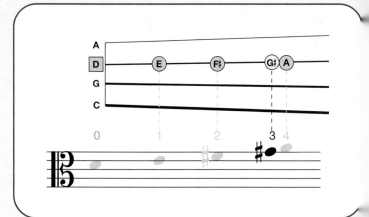

G# on the D string—3 Fingers Down
3–4 Pattern

42 *Aim High* CD 1:23

43 *Mary's Lamb*

SARAH JOSEPHA HALE, U.S.A.

mf

 Ear Training Expression—Worksheet #2

44 Extension Chord

Remember to roll your left elbow under the instrument.

 Creative Expression—Improvise using the I chord in D Major and passing tones (Worksheet #20)

45 Target Practice

46 Lamb Chops

(Based on "Mary Had a Little Lamb")

47 Another Extension Chord

48 Cross Walk

Lift and place fingers across strings for each note.

49 A Major Scale #1 and Arpeggio*

 **Orchestra @ Home**

LESSON 1

. Perform orchestra and vibrato warm-ups to CD 1:22.

. Perform Lines 42–44 and your favorite line that begins with C#-B-A. Focus on proper arm and hand positions in extensions.

. Improvise using Worksheet #20 and CD 1:57.

LESSON 2

1. Perform orchestra and vibrato warm-ups to CD 1:22.

2. Prepare Line 46 for individual assessment.

3. Perform Lines 43 and 46. Change the melody of Line 43 to create a variation.

LESSON 3

1. Perform orchestra and vibrato warm-ups to CD 1:22.

2. Perform Line 48. Explain the cross-string note relationships to family and friends.

3. Practice Line 49 using Rhythm Chart #6.

Warm-ups CD 1:22

Creative Tools of Music

A Tempo—return to the previous tempo

🐢 **Fermata**—hold a note or rest longer than its value

Ritardando (ritard., rit.)—gradually slow down

Review Finger Patterns

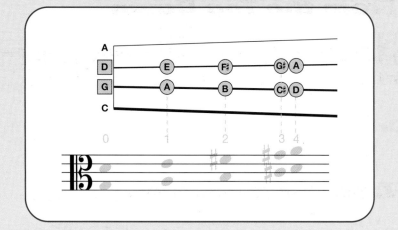

50 Los Pollitos CD 1:25

Moderato

Folk Song, Ecuador

51 Chester* CD 1:26

Moderato

WILLIAM BILLINGS, U.S.A.

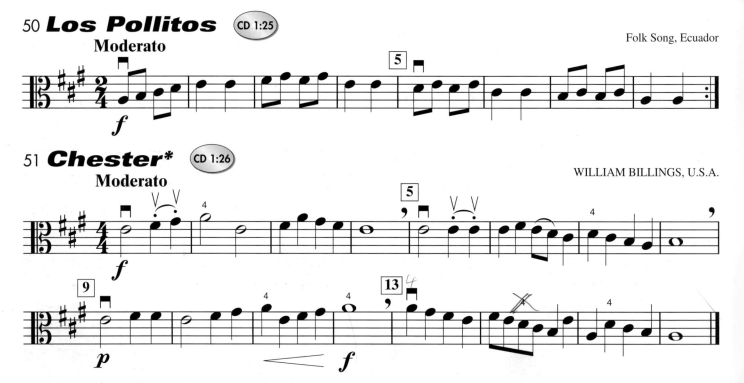

 Ear Training Expression—Worksheet #2

52 Shepherd's Hey* CD 1:27

Allegro

Country Dance, England

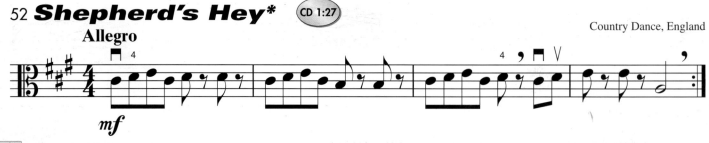

Creative Expression—Composition #3 (Worksheet #22)

53 Down Draft

Allegro

54 From the Top Down

55 A Major Scale #2 and Arpeggio*

56 A Twinkle in Your Eye

Based on a Folk Song, France

57 Stretch Limo CD 1:28

GERALD ANDERSON, U.S.A.

Orchestra @ Home

LESSON 1

- Perform orchestra and vibrato warm-ups to CD 1:22.
- Practice Lines 50–51 using Tone Variables to create dynamics.
- Practice Line 52 for rhythmic and pitch accuracy.
- Complete your composition in A major.

LESSON 2

1. Perform orchestra and vibrato warm-ups to CD 1:22.
2. Practice Line 56 with the ritardando, fermata, and a tempo.
3. Practice, prepare, and perform Line 51 for family and friends.

LESSON 3

1. Perform orchestra and vibrato warm-ups to CD 1:22.
2. Practice Line 57. Focus on extensions and dotted rhythms.
3. Memorize Line 51, measures 1–8.
4. Perform Line 56 for family and friends.
5. Complete Worksheet #24 if more time is needed.

Warm-ups CD 1:22

Creative Tools of Music

Canon—a round in which each new voice enters after a specific amount of time

Ground Bass—a repeated pattern of notes in the lowest voice that supports all the voices above it

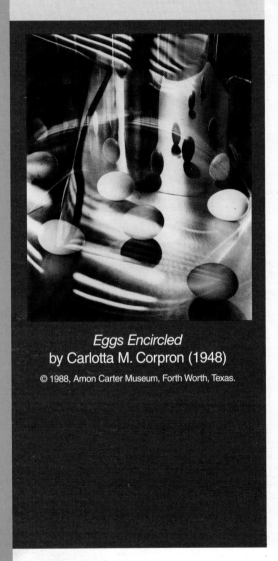

Eggs Encircled
by Carlotta M. Corpron (1948)

© 1988, Amon Carter Museum, Forth Worth, Texas.

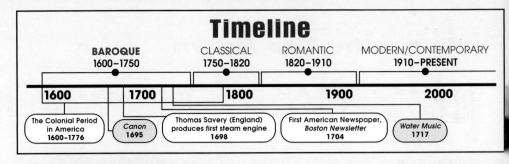

Timeline

BAROQUE 1600–1750	CLASSICAL 1750–1820	ROMANTIC 1820–1910	MODERN/CONTEMPORARY 1910–PRESENT

1600	1700	1800	1900	2000

The Colonial Period in America 1600–1776

Canon 1695

Thomas Savery (England) produces first steam engine 1698

First American Newspaper, *Boston Newsletter* 1704

Water Music 1717

PORTRAIT

Johann Pachelbel

Johann Pachelbel was born in Nuremberg, Germany in 1653 and lived there until his death in 1706. Because of his high academic abilities, he received a generous scholarship to a college-preparatory high school in Regensburg. Throughout his life he worked as a church organist and composed an enormous amount of choral and instrumental music. His influence as a music teacher can be seen by its effect on his children, one of whom was an organist in the American Colonies in 1730, and in one of the greatest musical families in history: the Bach family. Pachelbel was the teacher of Johann Christoph Bach, who in turn taught Johann Sebastian Bach. "Canon in D" is considered to be Pachelbel's most famous work.

Baroque Music

The term baroque applies to a style that was evident in the clothing, furniture, art, architecture, literature, and music of the time. Each of these was highly decorated with elaborate ornamentation. Rhythmic energy, improvisation, and ornamentation were characteristics of the baroque style of music.

New Finger Pattern on the C String

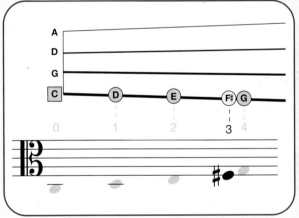

F♯ on the C string—
3 Fingers Down
3–4 Pattern

 Ear Training Expression—Worksheet #2

58 Bull's Eye CD 1:29

59 Field Goal

60 D Major Scale and Arpeggio*

61 Oh! Susanna

CD 1:30

STEPHEN COLLINS FOSTER, U.S.A.

62 Canon*

CD 1:31

(Orchestra Arrangement)

JOHANN PACHELBEL, Germany
Arranged by SANDRA DACKOW, U.S.A.

Largo

Creative Expression—Improvise over a Ground Bass (Worksheet #26)

 CD 1:32

Orchestra @ Home

LESSON 1

. Perform orchestra and vibrato warm-ups to CD 1:22.

. Practice Lines 60–61. Focus on extended finger patterns.

. Learn Line 62. Explain the Music History Timeline to family and friends.

. Memorize all of Line 51.

. Play by ear the music from TV shows or commercials.

LESSON 2

1. Perform orchestra and vibrato warm-ups to CD 1:22.

2. Practice and prepare Line 61. Focus on intonation and rhythm.

3. Teach what you learned about Pachelbel and Baroque music to family and friends.

LESSON 3

1. Perform orchestra and vibrato warm-ups to CD 1:22.

2. Perform your favorite memorized pieces.

3. Play CD 1:22 for family or friends, and ask them where they have heard it before. Improvise over the ground bass. CD 1:32

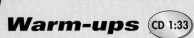

Creative Tools of Music

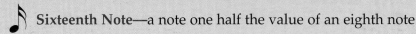

Sixteenth Note—a note one half the value of an eighth note

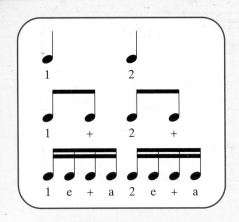

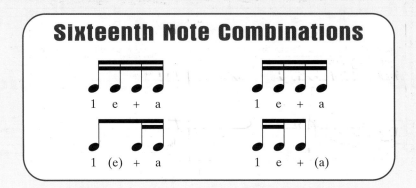

63 Mississippi Steamboat

64 The Hopeful Lover CD 1:34

Fiddle Tune, Scotland

65 The Lost Lover CD 1:35

GERALD ANDERSON, U.S.A.

66 Perpetual Motion

Use an energetic bow stroke.

67 Black Diamond Reel* CD 1:36

GERALD ANDERSON, U.S.A.

Creative Expression—Arrangement #2 (Worksheet #28)

68 Grasshopper Hoppergrass

1 e + a 2 e + a

1 (e) + a 2 (e) + a

1 e + (a) 2 e + (a)

69 Sailor's Song* CD 1:37

Sea Shanty, England

Allegro

mf   *cresc.*

 Ear Training Expression—Worksheet #2

70 Jim Along Josie CD 1:38

Words and Music by
EDWARD HARPER, U.S.A.

Allegro

f

71 Laughing (Round)

Folk Song, Germany

Moderato

mp   *cresc.*   *f*   *mp*   *f*   *mp*

Orchestra @ Home

LESSON 1

1. Perform orchestra and vibrato warm-ups to CD 1:33.

2. Practice Lines 63–65 counting all rhythms carefully. Use fast, energetic bow speeds. Explain how to count sixteenth and eighth notes to family and friends.

LESSON 2

. Perform orchestra and vibrato warm-ups to CD 1:33.

. Practice Line 66 using energetic sixteenth-note bowing. Observe all repeats.

3. Practice and perform Line 67. Teach what you learned about a reel to family and friends.

4. Work on Worksheet #28.

LESSON 3

1. Perform orchestra and vibrato warm-ups to CD 1:33.

2. Practice Parts 1 and 2 of Line 68. Count the rhythm aloud.

3. Practice Line 69. Focus on rhythm, energetic playing, and the crescendo.

4. Complete Worksheet #28.

5. Practice and prepare Line 67. Focus on rhythmic accuracy, bow speed, and good intonation.

LESSON 4

1. Perform orchestra and vibrato warm-ups to CD 1:33.

2. Perform three lines from Unit 11, and explain something special about each piece.

3. Practice Line 71. Focus on how dynamics shape the question and answer parts of the phrase.

Warm-ups (CD 1:33)

Creative Tools of Music

Serenade—originally, a form of easy-listening music, usually performed out-of-doors in the evening or at a party; a musical valentine

Spiccato—a bouncing bow stroke; **heavy spiccato** is played in the lower half of the bow near the frog; **light spiccato** is a short bow stroke played near the balance point

The Love Song
by Alexei Stiepanoff
Photo Credit: Fine Art Photographic Library,
London/Art Resource, NY.

PORTRAIT

Pyotr Il'yich Tchaikovsky

Pyotr Il'yich Tchaikovsky was a Russian composer born in 1840 in a small industrial town about 600 miles from Moscow. He died in St. Petersburg, Russia in 1893. In English, Pyotr is translated as Peter. Tchaikovsky's middle name means "son of Ilya," Tchaikovsky's father. He studied law, but as an adult he entered a music conservatory for serious music study. Tchaikovsky was moody and often depressed, even though he was one of the most famous composers of his day. In 1891, he traveled to America to conduct the opening concert of Carnegie Hall in New York City. Using Russian folk songs in his music, he wrote many operas and symphonies, but Tchaikovsky is especially beloved for his three ballets: *The Nutcracker*, *Sleeping Beauty* and *Swan Lake*. His *Serenade for Strings* is a favorite with string players everywhere, although he may be best known for his *1812 Overture*, written in 1880 for the Moscow Exhibition.

Look at the **Romantic Period** Timeline in Unit #7 for *Serenade for Strings*.

72 *Basketball Dribble* (CD 1:39)

p–f

73 *Double Dribble*

p–f   *p–f*

74 *Scribble Dribble*

p–f   *p–f*   *p–f*

75 *Can Can**

JACQUES OFFENBACH, France

Allegro

f

Ear Training Expression—Worksheet #2

76 Trepak* CD 1:41

Allegro

PYOTR IL'YICH TCHAIKOVSKY, Russia

77 Finale From Serenade for Strings CD 1:42

(Orchestra Arrangement)

PYOTR IL'YICH TCHAIKOVSKY, Russia
Arranged by SANDRA DACKOW, U.S.A.

Allegro

 Creative Expression—Improvise movement to "Finale" from *Serenade for Strings*

Orchestra @ Home

LESSON 1

1. Perform orchestra and vibrato warm-ups to CD 1:33.

2. Practice light staccato on open D. Focus on a relaxed bow hold and steady eighth notes in the bouncing spot.

3. Practice Lines 72–73. Focus on steady tempo and spiccato.

LESSON 2

1. Perform orchestra and vibrato warm-ups to CD 1:33.

2. Practice Lines 72–74 using light and heavy spiccato on each one.

3. Practice Line 75. Focus on heavy spiccato bowing and the correct bouncing point.

4. Learn Line 76 using the Sight-Reading Procedure. Use heavy spiccato.

LESSON 3

1. Perform orchestra and vibrato warm-ups to CD 1:33.

2. Practice Lines 75–77. Focus on proper spiccato style.

3. Teach what you learned about Tchaikovsky and his ballets to family and friends.

23

Warm-ups CD 1:43

Creative Tools of Music

> Accent—start the note with emphasis

78 **Accent!** CD 1:44

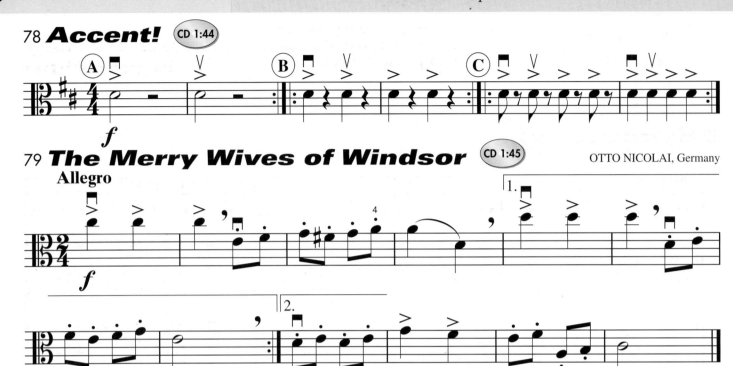

79 **The Merry Wives of Windsor** CD 1:45

OTTO NICOLAI, Germany

Allegro

Creative Expression—Arrangement #3 (Worksheet #31)

80 **Anvil Chorus*** CD 1:46

GIUSEPPE VERDI, Italy

Moderato

81 **Accent on a Rock**

GERALD ANDERSON, U.S.A.

Allegro

Ear Training Expression—Worksheet #2

Orchestra @ Home

LESSON 1

1. Perform orchestra and vibrato warm-ups to CD 1:43.

2. Practice Lines 78–79. Focus on accents. Remember to hook, release, and stop each accented note.

3. Complete your arrangement.

LESSON 2

1. Perform orchestra and vibrato warm-ups to CD 1:43.

2. Practice and prepare Lines 79–80. Focus on accents. Teach what you learned about accents in opera music to family and friends.

3. Practice Line 81. Focus on placing the bow after the lift for a firm accent.

4. Practice and prepare your arrangement.

LESSON 3

1. Perform orchestra and vibrato warm-ups to CD 1:43.

2. Practice Lines 79–81 refining the use of accents.

3. Perform your arrangement for family and friends.

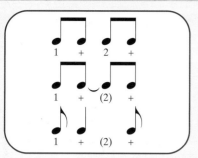

Creative Tools of Music

Syncopation—a rhythm with the emphasis on a weak beat or weak portion of a beat

Ear Training Expression—
Worksheet #2

82 Syncopation

83 Lil' Liza Jane CD 1:47

Allegro

COUNTESS ADA DELACHAU, U.S.A.

84 Shake the Papaya Down CD 1:48

Moderato

Folk Song, Jamaica

85 Meet the Flintstones CD 1:49

Allegro

Words and Music by
WILLIAM HANNA, JOSEPH BARBERA, and
HOYT CURTIN, U.S.A.

Creative Expression—Improvise over the I and V chords in D Major
(Worksheet #36)

CD 1:59

Orchestra @ Home Your teacher will give you your lesson assignment.

UNIT 15 • Rhythm: ♪♪♪

Warm-ups (CD 1:43)

Creative Tools of Music

Hornpipe—a lively folk dance of the British Isles originally accompanied by hornpipe playing

Deluge 1980
by Gail Butt (b. 1924)
Reprinted with the artist's permission.

Look at the **Baroque Period** Timeline in Unit #10 for *Water Music*.

George Frideric Handel

George Frideric Handel was born in Halle, Germany in 1685, and died in London, England in 1759. In his early years he studied the organ, harpsichord, oboe, and violin. He traveled widely in Italy and England, soaking up musical influences and blending them into a style uniquely his own. His music was often performed for the parties and court functions of King George I of England. He settled in England and was much beloved for his pleasing melodies. As his compositions were in high demand, he often simply rearranged his music when time did not permit him to write something new. Handel wrote so much music that he, like Bach, went blind from the eyestrain. Handel wrote keyboard, vocal, choral, orchestral, and chamber music, including *Music for the Royal Fireworks* and *Water Music*. He also composed operas and oratorios, including his famous oratorio, *Messiah*.

86 Kang Ding Qing Ge (CD 1:50)

Moderato — Folk Song, China

87 Cheki Morena (CD 1:51)

Allegro — Folk Song, Puerto Rico

88 Caissons Go Rolling Along (CD 1:52)

Allegro — EDMUND L. GRUBER, U.S.A.

26

89 You're a Grand Old Flag* CD 1:53
Moderato

Words and Music by
GEORGE M. COHAN, U.S.A.

90 Hornpipe From "Water Music" CD 1:54
(Orchestra Arrangement)

GEORGE FRIDERIC HANDEL, Germany, England
Arranged by SANDRA DACKOW, U.S.A.

Moderato

  Creative Expression—Improvise Movement to "Hornpipe" from *Water Music*

 **Ear Training Expression**—Worksheet #2

Orchestra @ Home

LESSON 1
1. Perform orchestra and vibrato warm-ups to CD 1:43.
2. Practice Lines 86–87. Focus on rhythm and hooked bowing in the syncopation.

LESSON 2
1. Perform orchestra and vibrato warm-ups to CD 1:43.
2. Practice Lines 88–89. Focus on accents and hooked bowing.

3. Teach what you learned about the Army anthem to family and friends.

LESSON 3
1. Perform orchestra and vibrato warm-ups to CD 1:43.
2. Practice the melody of Line 90. Play slowly perfecting the bowing, rhythms, accents, and intonation. Teach someone what you learned about the king's boating party.
3. Learn the orchestra part for Line 90. Find rhythms similar to the melody.

4. Perform Line 89. Teach someone what you have learned about this piece.

LESSON 4
1. Perform orchestra and vibrato warm-ups to CD 1:43.
2. Practice and prepare Line 89. Focus on hooked bowing and changing pitches.
3. Practice all parts of Line 90.

UNITS 16–18 WILL BE PRESENTED BY YOUR TEACHER.

27

Warm-ups CD 2:3

Key of F Major

Rhythm Chart 7

A.
B.
C.
D.

Creative Tools of Music

♭ **Flat**—a symbol that lowers the pitch of a note one half step

Harmonic—a high, flutelike tone produced by lightly touching the string in certain places with a left-hand finger while bowing

New Finger Pattern on the A String

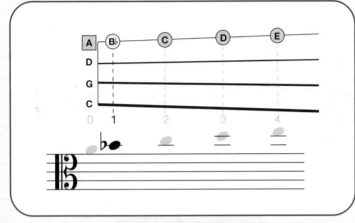

New Note B♭ on the G String

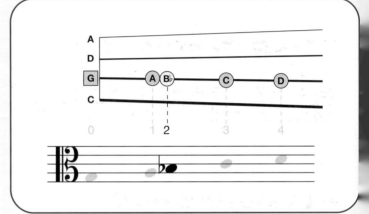

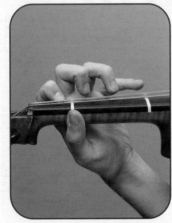

B♭ on the A string—
1 Finger Down
1 2 3 4 Open Pattern

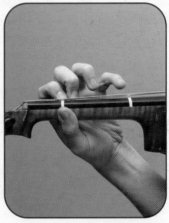

B♭ on the G string—
2 Fingers Down
1-2 Pattern

91 **Bee Flat Bug Spray** CD 2:4

92 **Lamb Chop's B-a-a-d Variation**
(Based on "Mary Had a Little Lamb")

Based on a Folk Song, U.S.A.

93 Bee Flat Stinger

94 Red Beans and Rice CD 2:5

GERALD ANDERSON, U.S.A.

95 Frog Hollow CD 2:6

Lift fingers as you cross strings.

96 Crawfish Boil

97 F Major Scale and Arpeggio*

Ear Training Expression—Worksheet #2

Orchestra @ Home

LESSON 1

1. Perform orchestra and vibrato warm-ups to CD 2:3.

2. Practice extended first finger movement.

3. Practice Lines 91–92 with good intonation and finger patterns.

4. Practice Line 93. Focus on the G string finger pattern.

5. Practice Line 94 with good intonation and rhythm.

LESSON 2

1. Perform orchestra and vibrato warm-ups to CD 2:3.

2. Practice Lines 91 and 93. Focus on correct finger patterns.

3. Practice Lines 95–96. Focus on cross-string relationships and cleanly lifting the fingers.

4. Practice Line 97 using Rhythm Chart #7.

LESSON 3

1. Perform orchestra and vibrato warm-ups to CD 2:3.

2. Practice Lines 91 and 93. Focus on intonation and finger patterns.

3. Practice Line 97 using Rhythm Chart #7.

4. Perform Line 94. Explain to family and friends what you learned about Cajun cooking and zydeco music.

Warm-ups CD 2:3

✎ **Ear Training Expression**—Worksheet #2

98 *Waltzing Matilda* CD 2:7

Words by A. B. "BANJO" PATTERSON, Australia
Music by MARIE COWAN, Australia

99 *Sea Shanty* * CD 2:8
(Blow the Man Down)

Sea Shanty, England

100 *The Yellow Rose of Texas* CD 2:9

Folk Song, U.S.A.

Keep 4th finger down.

💡 **Creative Expression**—Composition #5 (Worksheet #46)

 Orchestra @ Home

LESSON 1

1. Perform orchestra and vibrato warm-ups to CD 2:3.

2. Practice Lines 98–100. Focus on intonation and finger patterns.

3. Work on your composition.

4. Prepare Line 97 for assessment. Focus on good intonation.

LESSON 2

1. Perform orchestra and vibrato warm-ups to CD 2:3.

2. Practice Lines 98–100. Focus on good intonation, and correct finger patterns, bowings, and rhythms.

3. Perform a concert for family and friends of Lines 98–100.

Creative Tools of Music

Minor Key—a key in which the 3rd, 6th, and 7th steps of the scale are one half step lower than in a major scale

Relative Scales—major and minor scales that have the same key signature but begin on different notes

Creative Expression—Composition #6
(Worksheet #49)

Ear Training Expression—Worksheet #2

Key of D minor

101 D Minor Scale and Arpeggio*

102 Night in the Desert   CD 2:10

Moderato

Folk Song, Arabia

mp

103 Shalom Chaverim (Round)

Moderato

Folk Song, Israel

104 Little Apple*

Moderato

Folk Song, Russia

Orchestra @ Home

LESSON 1

1. Perform orchestra and vibrato warm-ups to CD 2:3.

2. Practice Lines 101–103. Focus on good intonation.

3. Complete your composition.

LESSON 2

1. Perform orchestra and vibrato warm-ups to CD 2:3.

2. Practice Line 101. Focus on intonation.

3. Practice Lines 103 and 104. Focus on intonation and the use of tone variables to create dynamics.

LESSON 3

1. Perform orchestra and vibrato warm-ups to CD 2:3.

2. Play all music lines on page 31. Focus on intonation, tone variables, and vibrato.

3. Practice your composition for performance at the next lesson.

UNIT 22 • Key: D Minor

Warm-ups CD 2:3

Creative Tools of Music

- **Coda**—an ending section of music
- **Dal Segno (D.S.)**—repeat a section of music beginning at the sign
- **D.S. al Coda**—repeat from the sign, go to the coda symbol, and play the coda to the end
- **Overture**—a composition for orchestra often written as an introduction to an opera; it may contain some of the main musical themes of the opera

Look at the **Romantic Period** Timeline in Unit #7 for *William Tell Overture*.

Illustration to "Wilhelm Tell"
by Friedrich Schiller (1805)
Photo Credit: Bildarchiv Preussischer Kulturbesitz/Art Resource, NY

PORTRAIT

Gioachino Rossini

Gioachino Rossini was born in Pesaro, Italy, in 1792 and died in Paris, France in 1868. His parents were both professionally involved in the local opera theater. He studied several musical instruments and composed for them at a very young age, but it was as an opera composer that he would eventually become famous. Rossini gave the world some of its most delightful comic opera. He could write at an amazing speed and still produce wonderful music. One of his most famous operas, *The Barber of Seville*, was written in only 13 days! *William Tell* was a serious French Grand opera and was the last he wrote. One of Rossini's great interests was cooking (and eating!). He created several recipes that became popular and still carry his name today.

William Tell

William Tell was a thirteenth-century, Swiss patriot when Austria ruled Switzerland. An evil Austrian governor named Gessler raised his hat on a flagpole in the marketplace and ordered all to bow down and salute his hat as a symbol of obedience to him. All bowed but William Tell, who had come to the market with his young son. Gessler arrested Tell and ordered him to shoot an apple off the head of his son from across the market square. Tell took aim with his crossbow and arrow and shot the apple through the core. Gessler noticed a second arrow in Tell's quiver. "That was for you in case I missed," Tell said to Gessler. Furious, Gessler ordered Tell to be arrested, but the Swiss people rose in defiance, marking the beginning of the Swiss liberation and the fall of Gessler.

105 Three Red Roses CD 2:11

Folk Song, Ukraine

Allegro

Ear Training Expression—Worksheet #2

Creative Expression—Create movement to *William Tell (Theme From the Overture)*

106 **William Tell** CD 2:12
(Theme From the Overture)

GIOACCHINO ROSSINI, Italy
Arranged by SANDRA DACKOW, U.S.A.

Allegro

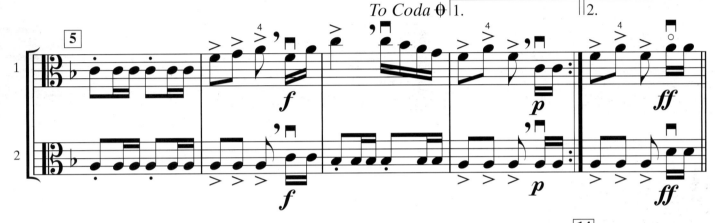

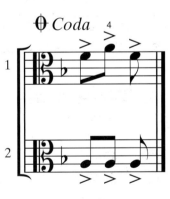

Orchestra @ Home

LESSON 1

1. Perform orchestra and vibrato warm-ups to CD 2:3.

2. Practice Line 105. Focus on intonation, rhythms, and dynamics.

3. Practice 1 and 2 parts of Line 106. Observe accidentals and the D.S. al Coda.

LESSON 2

1. Perform orchestra and vibrato warm-ups to CD 2:3.

2. Practice Line 105. Focus on intonation, rhythms, and dynamics.

3. Practice both parts of Line 106. Observe accidentals and the D.S. al Coda.

LESSON 3

1. Perform orchestra and vibrato warm-ups to CD 2:3.

2. Perform the melody of Line 106 with the CD. Explain the opera's plot to family and friends.

3. Extra Credit: Check out and listen to a library recording of the complete "Overture" to *William Tell*.

Warm-ups CD 2:13

Key of B♭ Major

Rhythm Chart 8

A. ♩ = ♪ ♪

B. ♩ = ♬♬

C. ♩ = ♪ ♬

D. ♩ = ♬ ♪

New Finger Pattern on the D String

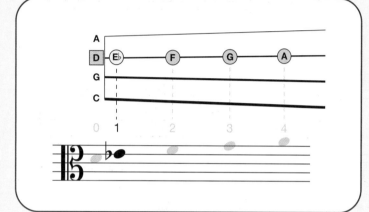

New Finger Pattern on the A String

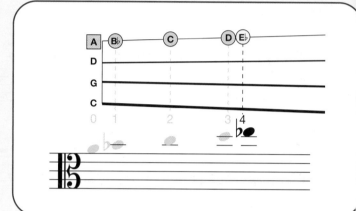

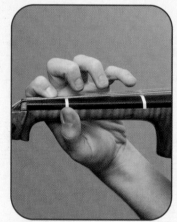

E♭ on the D string—
1 Finger Down
1 2 3 4 Open Pattern

E♭ on the A string—
4 Fingers Down
3-4 Pattern

107 Push 'Em Back CD 2:14

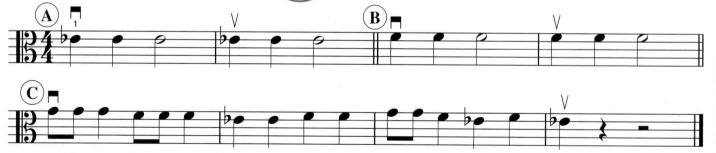

108 A Lamb in Wolf's Clothing

(Based on "Mary Had a Little Lamb")

Warm-ups CD 2:13

Creative Tools of Music

Solo—music to be performed by one person
Tutti—music to be performed by everyone

Ear Training Expression—Worksheet #2

117 Ein Keiloheinu CD 2:18

Moderato

Traditional Hebrew Song

118 Che Che Koolay

Moderato

Singing Game, Ghana

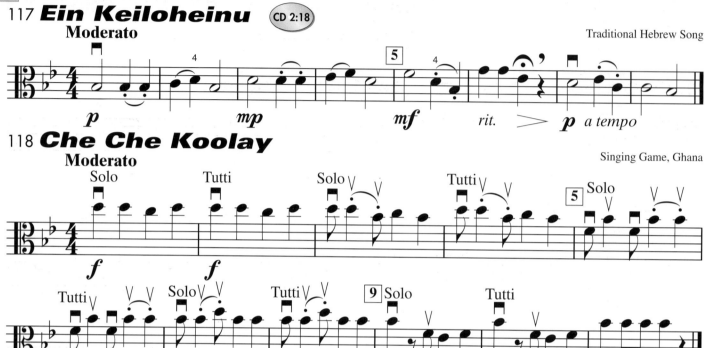

Creative Expression—Composition #7 (Worksheet #54A, B, C)

119 Turkish March* CD 2:19

Moderato

LUDWIG VAN BEETHOVEN, Germany, Austria

120 The Blue Bells of Scotland CD 2:20

Andante

Folk Song, Scotland

Orchestra @ Home Your teacher will give you your lesson assignment.

Creative Tools of Music

+ Left Hand Pizzicato—use the fingers of the left hand to play pizzicato

Key of G minor

Refer back to the Tone Variables Chart in Unit 1, page 2 to help with expressive dynamics.

121 G Minor Scale #1 and Arpeggio*

122 Siciliano

Andante

JOHANN SEBASTIAN BACH, Germany

Creative Expression—Composition #8 (Worksheet #57A, B, C)

123 G Minor Scale #2 and Arpeggio*

124 The Little Birch Tree CD 2:21

Allegro

Folk Song, Russia

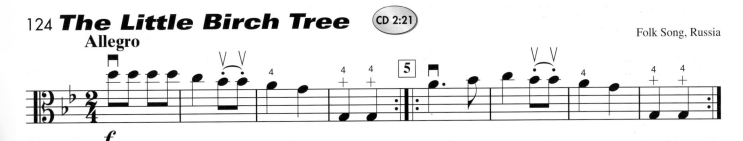

Ear Training Expression—Worksheet #2

Orchestra @ Home Your teacher will give you your lesson assignment.

37

Warm-ups CD 2:13

Creative Tools of Music

Parallel Scales—major and minor scales that begin on the same pitch but have different key signatures

Sonata-Allegro Form—a form of composition that has three sections: Exposition, Development, and Recapitulation

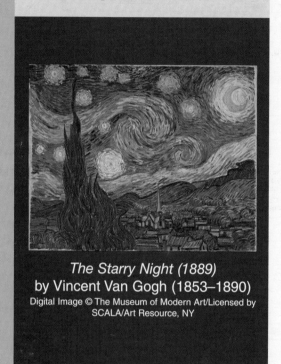

The Starry Night (1889)
by Vincent Van Gogh (1853–1890)
Digital Image © The Museum of Modern Art/Licensed by
SCALA/Art Resource, NY

Timeline

| BAROQUE 1600–1750 | CLASSICAL 1750–1820 | ROMANTIC 1820–1910 | MODERN/CONTEMPORARY 1910–PRESENT |

1600   1700   1800   1900   2000

American Declaration of Independence 1776

Eine Kleine Natchtmusik 1787

George Washington, 1st U.S. President 1789

PORTRAIT

WOLFGANG AMADEUS MOZART

One of the most extraordinary composers of all time, Wolfgang Amadeus Mozart was born in 1756 in Salzburg, Austria and died in Vienna in 1791. A child prodigy, Mozart studied the keyboard instruments of piano, organ, and harpsichord, and also the violin. A prodigy is someone who does amazing things at a young age. His earliest compositions were written when he was only eight. Mozart never attended school as a boy, but traveled widely as a young performer and learned to speak several languages. Traveling by horse-drawn carriage he visited distant cities such as London, Paris, Prague, Mannheim, and Bologna. As an adult, he also enjoyed playing the viola in small instrumental groups with other composers who were his friends. Mozart wrote very quickly and rarely made any changes. The number of his compositions totals over 800. He wrote operas, solos, concertos, symphonies, church music, and a great deal of chamber music.

Classical Music

During the Classical Period, many of the rough edges and irregularities found in Baroque music were smoothed out. Phrases became more regular and some of the wide leaps or intervals in both the melody and accompanying parts were replaced with elegant musical lines. There is a sense of balance and grace in Classical music. Music from this period is usually predictable and unsurprising. Famous composers of Classical music include Mozart, Haydn, and Beethoven in his early years. Most Classical composers were employed by Royalty and the wealthy families of Europe, who took great pride in their support of the arts.

125 Come Back to Sorrento*   CD 2:22

ERNESTO de CURTIS, Italy

Creative Expression—Theory (Worksheet #59A, B, C)

Ear Training Expression—Worksheet #2

126 **Allegro From "Eine Kleine Nachtmusik"*** CD 2:23
(Orchestra Arrangement)

WOLFGANG AMADEUS MOZART, Austria
Arranged by SANDRA DACKOW, U.S.A.

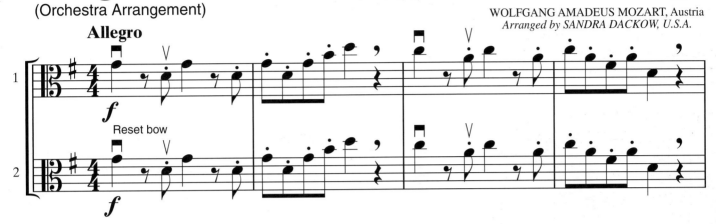

Creative Expression—Improvise a Call-and-response

Orchestra @ Home

LESSON 1

1. Perform orchestra and vibrato warm-ups to CD 2:13.

2. Practice Line 121. Focus on intonation and finger patterns.

3. Practice Line 125. Focus on key changes and adjust finger patterns for good intonation.

LESSON 2

1. Perform orchestra and vibrato warm-ups to CD 2:13.

2. Perform Line 125 with dynamics and a beautiful tone.

3. Practice the melody of Line 126. Focus on bowing and learn the orchestra part.

4. Teach someone what you know about Mozart.

LESSON 3

1. Perform orchestra and vibrato warm-ups to CD 2:13.

2. Practice both parts of Line 126. Focus on bowing.

3. Research Mozart's full name and compare it to your own full name.

UNIT 27 • Rhythm:

Warm-ups CD 2:24

Performing the dotted eighth note–sixteenth note rhythm is easier if the forearm is used for the dotted eighth note, and the single sixteenth note is played with the wrist.

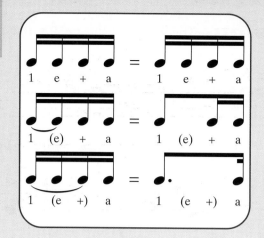

Creative Tools of Music

Dotted Eighth Note and Sixteenth Note—a rhythm counted as "1 (e +) a"

Dot—a dot after a note adds one half the value of the note

127 Day to Day

128 En el Lejano Bosque   CD 2:25

Folk Song, Spain

Moderato

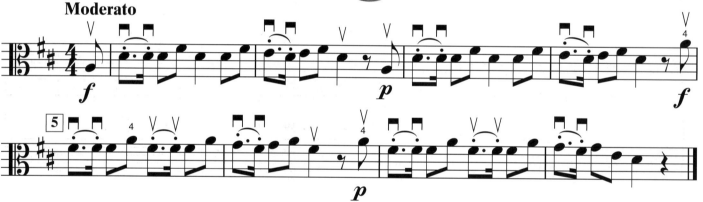

129 Off to War (Non Più Andrai)   CD 2:26

(From *Le Nozze di Figaro*/The Marriage of Figaro)

Allegro

WOLFGANG AMADEUS MOZART, Austria

 Ear Training Expression—Worksheet #2

 Creative Expression—Improvise over the IV chord in D Major (Worksheet #63)   CD 2:48

130 *Üsküdar* CD 2:27

Folk Song, Turkey

131 ***The Star-Spangled Banner****
(Orchestra Arrangement) CD 2:28

Music by JOHN STAFFORD SMITH, U.S.A.
Words by FRANCIS SCOTT KEY, U.S.A.
Arranged by SANDRA DACKOW, U.S.A.

rchestra @ Home Your teacher will give you your lesson assignment.

41

Warm-ups Creative Tools of Music

Barcarolle—a song or piece of instrumental music composed in a swaying 6/8 time (a "boat song" often associated with the gondoliers of Venice, Italy)

Slow 6/8 =
6 beats in a measure;
eighth note/rest receives one beat.

Fast 6/8
(count the same) =
2 beats in a measure;
dotted quarter note/rest receives one beat.

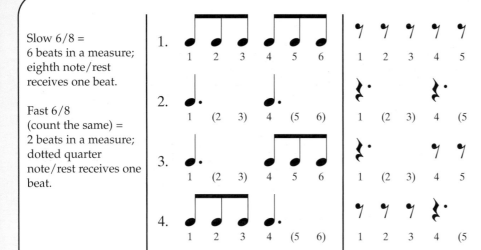

Conducting Patterns

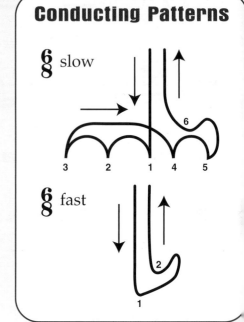

132 Deep Six

133 Hambani Kahle (Go Well and Safely) CD 2:29

Zulu Farewell, South Africa

Andante

mf

134 Scarborough Fair CD 2:30

Folk Song, England

Andante

mp

cresc.

mf

decresc.

mp

Ear Training Expression—Worksheet #2

135 **Barcarolle** CD 2:31

(From *The Tales of Hoffmann*)

JACQUES OFFENBACH, Italy and France

Creative Expression—Composition #9 (Worksheet #66)

136 **Lady, Lady** CD 2:32

Folk Song, England

137 **Vive la Compagnie*** CD 2:33

Folk Song, France

Reset bow

138 **Sweetly Sings the Donkey (Round)**

Folk Song, U.S.A.

Orchestra @ Home Your teacher will give you your lesson assignment.

Warm-ups CD 2:24

Creative Tools of Music

Malambo—a competitive dance characterized by high energy, virtuoso footwork, and heel tapping

Gauchos mounted on horses using bolas to hunt rhea, the flightless bird.
Credit: Image Select/Art Resource, NY

PORTRAIT

Alberto Ginastera

Alberto Ginastera was born in Buenos Aires, Argentina, in 1916 and died in Geneva, Switzerland in 1983. He started piano lessons at the age of seven and entered a conservatory when he was twelve. He studied composition in the United States and returned to Argentina to teach. He is celebrated for his use of Argentinean folk music and nationalistic subjects. He wrote ballets, operas, concertos, and various orchestral, vocal, and chamber works. The ballet, *Estancia*, written in 1941 for the American Ballet Caravan's tour of South America, is considered to be one of his finest works.

"Danza Final" From *Estancia*

An estancia is a large, ranch-like estate in Argentina. Large herds of cattle are worked by Argentinean cowboys called gauchos on the grasslands, or pampas, of these estates. Ginastera composed the ballet *Estancia* in 1941 to celebrate a love story set on such an estate. "Danza Final" concludes the ballet and is a competitive dance, called a malambo, for the gauchos. The malambo is characterized by high energy, virtuoso footwork, heel tapping, and a sense of competition among the dancers.

Look at the **Contemporary Period** Timeline in Unit #3 for *Estancia*.

139 *O Mio Babbino Caro* CD 2:34

(From *Gianni Schicchi*)

GIACOMO PUCCINI, Italy

140 When Johnny Comes Marching Home CD 2:35

PATRICK SARSFIELD GILMORE
(LOUIS LAMBERT), U.S.A.

 Ear Training Expression—Worksheet #2

141 The Irish Washerwoman* CD 2:36

Dance Tune, Ireland

142 Malambo CD 2:37

SANDRA DACKOW, U.S.A.

*Stomp feet: left-right-left.

Creative Expression—Improvise movement to "Danza Final"

Creative Expression—Theory (Worksheet #68)

rchestra @ Home Your teacher will give you your lesson assignment.

45

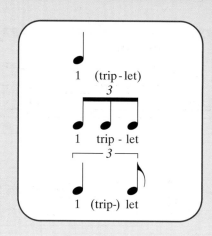

Warm-ups CD 2:38

Playing with a relaxed flexible wrist will allow the triplets to be played cleanly and accurately.

Creative Tools of Music

Chromatic—movement upward or downward by half-steps

Triplet—a rhythm of three notes played in the same time as two notes of the same value

143 Triplet Trio

144 Bowing Triplet Blues   CD 2:39

GERALD ANDERSON, U.S.A.

 Creative Expression—Composition #10 (Worksheet #71A, B, C)

 Ear Training Expression—Worksheet #2

Orchestra @ Home Your teacher will give you your lesson assignment.

46

145 **Ton-y-Botel** CD 2:40

Hymn Tune "Ebenezer"
Words by THOMAS JOHN WILLIAMS, Wales

Moderato

146 **Hang Gliding**

GERALD ANDERSON, U.S.A.

147 **Chromatic Colors**

148 **Habañera** CD 2:41

(From *Carmen*)
Andante

GEORGES BIZET, France

Warm-ups (CD 2:38)

Creative Tools of Music

¢ Cut Time—a time signature indicating two beats in a measure with a half note/rest receiving one beat

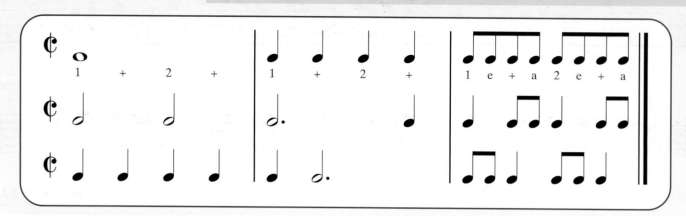

149 **Cutting Edge**

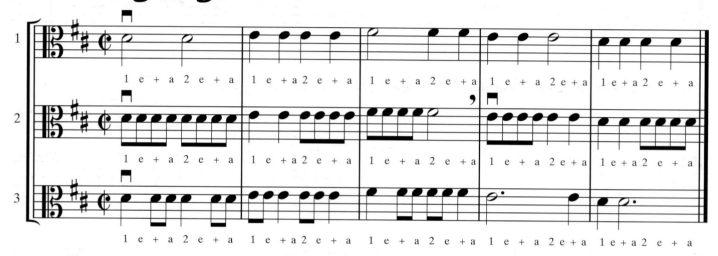

150 **Haak Gyo Jong** (CD 2:42)

Folk Song, Korea

Moderato

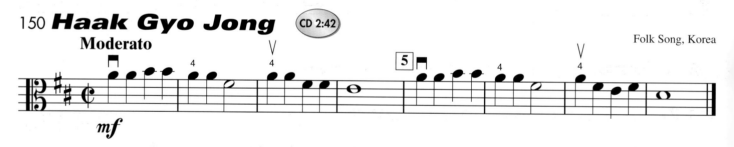

mf

151 **Crew Cut**

GERALD ANDERSON, U.S.A.

Allegro

mf

 Ear Training Expression—Worksheet #2

 Creative Expression—Improvise over the I, IV, V chords (Worksheet #75) (CD 2:49)

152 Cut the Mustard

Allegro

153 Skip to My Lou

Folk Song, U.S.A.

Allegro

154 When the Saints Go Marching In* CD 2:43

Traditional, U.S.A.
Words by KATHARINE E. PURVIS, U.S.A.
Music by JAMES M. BLACK, U.S.A.

Allegro

Reset bow   Reset bow

Reset bow

![pencil icon] **Ear Training Expression**—Worksheet #2

155 This Land Is Your Land* CD 2:44

Words and Music by
WOODY GUTHRIE, U.S.A.

Creative Expression—Improvise over "When the Saints Go Marching In"

Creative Expression—Improvise over the I, II, V chords (Worksheet #77) CD 2:50

rchestra @ Home Your teacher will give you your lesson assignment.

49

Warm-ups CD 2:38

Creative Tools of Music
Simile—play in the same style

Ear Training Expression—Worksheet #2

156 Batman Theme   CD 2:45
Allegro

Words and Music by
NEAL HEFTI, U.S.A.

This Arrangement © 2006 EMI MILLER CATALOG INC. All Rights Reserved

157 Over the Rainbow*   CD 2:46
Andante

Lyrics by E. Y. HARBURG, U.S.A.
Music by HAROLD ARLEN, U.S.A.

mf
Some - where   o - ver the rain - bow   way   up   high,   there's   a   land   that   I   heard   of
Some - where   o - ver the rain - bow   skies   are   blue,   and   the   dreams   that   you   dare   to

once   in   a   lul - la - by.   true.   *mp* Some - day   I'll   wish   up - on   a   star   and
dream   real - ly   do   come

wake   up   where   the   clouds   are   far   be - hind   me.   Where   trou - bles   melt   like   lem - on   drops, a -
mf   *mp*

Keep fingers down.
way   a - bove   the   chim - ney   tops,   that's   where   you'll   find   me.   Some - where   o - ver   the   rain - bow
cresc.   *f*   *mf*

blue - birds   fly.   Birds   fly   o - ver   the   rain - bow.   Why   then,   oh   why   can't   I?
mp

This Arrangement © 2006 METRO-GOLDWYN MAYER INC. and EMI FEIST CATALOG INC. All Rights Reserved

Orchestra @ Home Your teacher will give you your lesson assignment.

UNITS 34–36 WILL BE PRESENTED BY YOUR TEACHE

PORTRAIT

John Williams

John Williams was born in New York in 1932 and moved to Los Angeles with his family in 1948. He grew up in a musical atmosphere, as his father was a film studio musician. While he was in Los Angeles, he attended UCLA where he studied composition. After service in the Air Force, Williams returned to New York to study piano performance at the Juilliard School. He then returned to Los Angeles where he began his career as a composer of film music. Williams composed the music and served as music director for nearly eighty films, including "Saving Private Ryan," "Schindler's List," "Jurassic Park," "Home Alone," the "Indiana Jones" trilogy, the "Star Wars" trilogy, "E.T.: The Extra-Terrestrial," "Superman," "Close Encounters of the Third Kind," and "Jaws." The soundtrack to "Star Wars" has sold millions. In addition to many guest conducting appearances, Williams served as conductor of the Boston Pops Orchestra from 1980–1993.

COURTESY OF Lucasfilm Ltd.

Star Wars: Episode IV - A New Hope
© 1977 and 1997 Lucasfilm Ltd. & ™.

Look at the **Contemporary Period** Timeline in Unit #3 for *Star Wars*.

158 Star Wars

(Main Title)   CD 2:47

By **JOHN WILLIAMS**, U.S.A.
Arranged by MICHAEL STORY, U.S.A.

Creative Expression—Improvise the Blues (Worksheet #80)   CD 2:51

Play one pattern for each scale pitch

A. B. C. D. E.

F. G. H. I. J.

K. L. M. N. O.

Play one pattern for two scale pitches

P. Q. R.

Play one pattern for four scale pitches

S. T. U. V.

W. X. Y. Z.

C Major (Upper Octave)

C Major (Lower Octave)

G Major

D Major (Upper Octave)

D Major (Lower Octave)

A Major

F Major

Bb Major

A Minor

D Minor (Upper Octave)

D Minor (Lower Octave)

G Minor

VIBRATO WARM-UPS

- Your fingernails must be trimmed to the correct length to perform vibrato correctly.
- Perform the assigned vibrato exercises during the warm-up phase of your practice time at home.
- Keep the motion slow and relaxed.
- Stop when your shoulder, arm, wrist, or hand feels tight or tired.

GOOD-BYE! (Wrist Movement)

- Without the instrument, place your left arm in playing position with your palm facing you.
- Gently wave good-bye to yourself. Keep your arm still and wave only your hand from your wrist. The waving motion should be made equally backwards and forwards.

SHAKE! SHAKE! SHAKE! (Wrist Movement)

- While holding a shaker, place your left arm in playing position. Using the gentle wave good-bye motion, keep a steady rhythm with a shaker.
- Use the various vibrato rhythms provided at the bottom of this page.

STRING POLISHES (Wrist and Finger Movement)

- With the instrument in playing position, curve all fingers over the strings. You may use your right hand to support the instrument.
- Anchor your thumb in one location. Gently slide your second finger down and up the D string. Keep all other fingers curved. Do the same motion using third, fourth, and first fingers.
- You may use a piece of tissue to help your fingers slide more easily.
- Using each finger, polish the various vibrato rhythms provided at the bottom of this page.

FINGER SLIDES (Finger and Knuckle Movement)

- Anchor your thumb in one location. Your wrist should remain straight.
- Begin with first finger on the D string. Slide your finger from its curved position forward to a straight position and back to the curved position. The finger will move from the tip to the pad of the finger and back to the tip. Do this movement four times. Slide all individual fingers in this manner. Keep your fingers below the sliding finger anchored.

RHYTHMIC ROCKING (Finger, Knuckle, and Wrist Movement)

- With the instrument in playing position, curve all fingers over the strings.
- Begin String Polishes with your second finger on the D string. The polishing motion should become smaller and smaller until the finger is in one place on the string.
- Anchoring your second finger firmly on the D string, continue the rocking motion with your finger on the tip.
- Practice this exercise on each finger, moving from second, third, fourth, and first finger.
- Rock each finger with a steady motion to the vibrato rhythms.
- Shake out any tension when your shoulder, arm, wrist, or hand feels tight or tired.

VIBRATO RHYTHMS

- Begin these rhythms at ♩ = 60.
- Use each rhythm pattern, rest for one measure, and repeat several times.
- Gradually increase the speed as you master the exercises.
- Rest when your shoulder, arm, wrist, or hand feels tight or tired.
- ↑ means to move your hand backward; ↓ means to move your hand forward.

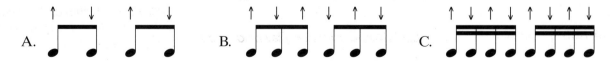

Glossary
Page numbers refer to the Student Book page where the definition is shown.

A Tempo—*return to the previous tempo (16)*

> Accent—*start the note with emphasis (24)*

Barcarolle—*a song or piece of instrumental music composed in a swaying 6/8 time (a "boat song" often associated with the gondoliers of Venice, Italy) (42)*

Bow Placement—*the placement of the bow on the string in relation to the frog or tip to change the volume: near the frog (f) near the tip (p); (2)*

Bow Speed—*the speed by which the bow is pulled across the string (increasing the bow speed can produce a louder sound; decreasing the bow speed can produce a softer sound): fast (f) or slow (p) (2)*

Bow Weight—*the amount of traction created by the bow as it is pulled across the string (increasing arm weight can produce a louder sound; decreasing arm weight can produce a softer sound): heavy (f) or light (p) (2)*

Canon—*a round in which each new voice enters after a specific amount of time (18)*

Chromatic—*movement upward or downward by half-steps (46)*

Coda—*an ending section of music (32)*

Crescendo (cresc.)—*play gradually louder (4)*

¢ Cut Time—*a time signature indicating two beats in a measure with a half note/rest receiving one beat (48)*

Dal Segno (D.S.)—*repeat a section of music beginning at the sign (32)*

D.S. al Coda—*repeat from the sign, go to the coda symbol, and play the coda to the end (32)*

Decrescendo (decresc.)—*play gradually softer (4)*

Diminuendo (dim.)—*same as decrescendo (4)*

Dot—*a dot after a note adds one half the value of the note (10, 40)*

Dotted Eighth Note and Sixteenth Note—*a rhythm counted as "1 (e +) a" (40)*

Dotted Quarter Note—*a note that receives one and a half beats of sound in 4/4, 3/4 or 2/4 time; (10)*

Dynamics—*terms or symbols used to notate a sound level or change of sound level (2)*

Eighth Note—*a note one half the value of a quarter note (8)*

Eighth Rest—*a rest one half the value of a quarter rest (8)*

Fermata—*hold a note or rest longer than its value (16)*

Flat—*a symbol that lowers the pitch of a note one half step (28)*

f Forte—*play loudly (2)*

Ground Bass—*a repeated pattern of notes in the lowest voice that supports all the voices above it (18)*

Harmonic—*a high, flutelike tone produced by lightly touching the string in certain places with a left-hand finger while bowing (28)*

Hornpipe—*a lively folk dance of the British Isles originally accompanied by hornpipe playing (26)*

Interval—*the distance between two pitches (2)*

Key Signature—*indicates what notes are to be played with sharps or flats throughout the piece of music (-)*

Largo—*a very slow tempo (12)*

+ Left Hand Pizzicato—*use the fingers of the left hand to play pizzicato (36)*

Major Key—*a key in which the ascending step pattern of the scale is whole, whole, half, whole, whole, whole, half (-)*

Malambo—*a competitive dance characterized by high energy, virtuoso footwork, and heel tapping (44)*

mf Mezzo Forte—*play moderately loudly; softer than forte (4)*

mp Mezzo Piano—*play moderately softly; louder than piano (4)*

Minor Key—*a key in which the 3rd, 6th, and 7th steps of the scale are a half step lower than in a major scale (31)*

Overture—*a composition for orchestra often written as an introduction to an opera; it may contain some of the main musical themes of the opera (32)*

Parallel Scales—*major and minor scales that begin on the same pitch but have different key signatures (38)*

p Piano—*play softly (2)*

Relative Scales—*major and minor scales that have the same key signature but begin on different notes (31)*

Ritardando (ritard., rit.)—*gradually slow down (16)*

Sea Shanty—*a song sung by sailors as they worked (21)*

Serenade—*originally, a form of easy listening music, usually performed out-of-doors in the evening or at a party; a musical valentine (22)*

Simile—*play in the same style (50)*

Sixteenth Note—*a note one half the value of an eighth note (20)*

Solo—*music to be performed by one person (36)*

Sonata-Allegro Form—*a form of composition that has three sections: Exposition, Development, and Recapitulation (38)*

Sound Point—*the placement of the bow on the string in relation to the bridge to change the volume: near the bridge (f); near the fingerboard (p) (2)*

Spiccato—*a bouncing bow stroke;* **heavy spiccato** *is played in the lower half of the bow near the frog;* **light spiccato** *is a short bow stroke played near the balance point (22)*

Suite—*a collection of musical movements or dances (6)*

Syncopation—*a rhythm with the emphasis on a weak beat or weak portion of a beat (25)*

Time Signature—*a symbol at the beginning of the staff, indicating how many beats are in each measure and what kind of note or rest receives one beat (-)*

Triplet—*a rhythm of three notes played in the same time as two notes of the same value (46)*

Tutti—*music to be performed by everyone (36)*

Variation—*a musical form; a restatement that retains some features of the original idea or theme (8)*

Vibrato—*a technique for vibrating the sound to create a warm, rich tone (2)*

Index